The Writing Prompts Workbook, Grades 9-10: Story Starters for Journals, Assignments and More

Bryan Cohen

Edited by Debra Cohen and Amy Crater.

Copyright © 2012 Build Creative Writing Ideas and Bryan Cohen

All rights reserved.

ISBN: 0985482249
ISBN-13: 978-0-9854822-4-4

DEDICATION

I dedicate this book to all of my teachers at Upper Dublin High School who prepared me not just for writing papers in college but for a lifetime of writing.

CONTENTS

Introduction   i

1   Science Fiction   1

2   Health   6

3   Horror   9

4   High School   14

5   Personal Prompts   19

6   Fiction Prompts   24

7   Celebrity   29

8   Summer   34

9   School Days   39

10   Travel   44

11   Mystery   50

12   Family   55

13   Friendship   65

14   Writing   72

15   Acting   82

16   Wrestling   88

17   The American Dream   94

18   The Paranormal   99

Extra Page   101

About the Author   103

INTRODUCTION

Welcome to *The Writing Prompts Workbook*! Within these pages you'll find 200 writing prompts, two on each page, that will help to stimulate the imagination of your students or children. I've found that the key to allowing students to fully latch onto an idea is to give them a scenario followed by a question. In answering the question, young writers can take the same prompt a million different directions. You may even want to try photocopying a page and have your writers take on the same prompt at the beginning and the end of a school year just to see how different their storytelling has become.

The Writing Prompts Workbook series is a collection of books I've created after seeing how many parents and teachers have visited my website, Build Creative Writing Ideas (located at http://www.build-creative-writing-ideas.com). I have adapted my thousands of prompts into six workbooks designed to take a first grader creatively all the way up through the end of high school. The six books are available for grades 1-2, 3-4, 5-6, 7-8, 9-10 and 11-12. The prompts become more complex with each volume, but continue to remain imaginative and creative throughout.

I love hearing about the progress of students on my site and I'm always interested in hearing new ideas for delivering creative writing prompts to writers from the ages of five to 105. Feel free to contact me on my website for any questions and comments you can think of. I hope you and your future best-selling authors thoroughly enjoy this and future books in the series. Happy writing!

Sincerely,
Bryan Cohen
Author of *The Writing Prompts Workbook* Series

PS: While there is space below each prompt for your budding writers to write, there is a good chance they may have more to say than they can fit on the page. There is an extra page in the back if you'd like to photocopy it, but I strongly suggest that you also get a notebook and some extra pencils just in case. A dictionary for challenging words may also be helpful.

Name _____ Date _____

1. It's an alien invasion! You are one of the first people to make contact with a new alien species. Are you able to communicate? How does everything go? Talk about the experience and the aftermath.

2. Your family, friends, and life might be a lot different...if they were in space! Imagine that everything you knew was transported to a traveling space ship. How would your day to day life change?

Name _____ Date _____

3. In a world greatly enhanced by new technologies (that are being developed every day) you have come up with a world-changing device that could change life as we know it. What is the device and why does it make such an impact?

4. During an archaeological dig, a new species of intelligent life has been found deep within our own planet. You have been chosen to lead the expedition with a crack team of special ops and scientists. What do you find in there and how do you interact with this new form of life?

Name _____ Date _____

5. You have been transported to another dimension! This world is similar to our own, but several key things are different. What are these key things, how did you get there, and how might you be able to get home (if you even wanted to)?

6. Several warriors from the future have come back to stop a horrible event in the past from happening. They will wait out their entire lifetimes to ensure that the problem doesn't occur. And they live in your neighborhood. How do you interact with these warriors and do you take on their request for help?

Name _____ Date _____

7. Strange weather patterns begin to form on the planet earth. You are a police officer working your shift when a man comes in and confesses to causing these weather problems. He also says that he's not sure if he can stop it. Do you believe the man? How do you two stop the problem if it's even possible?

8. While watching television you realize that the characters on the screen are talking to you. You step close enough and you are sucked into the TV set. You are now in the shows that you love and watch. What, however, happens when the shows end? Are you able to get back to the real world?

Name _____ Date _____

9. Imagine a world in which many different alien races are
acquainted with each other and all of them live on a giant space station together. What is
your role on this station and how does the interaction go for you?

10. Robots have become the new best pet! You, like most people, have a robot and while
you aren't sure, it's possible that your particular pet has gained consciousness. You want to
tell someone, but you are afraid that something bad will happen to your robot as a result.
What do you do?

Name _____ Date _____

11. There are so many reports of deaths, injuries, and illnesses on the
news; it sometimes feels like we're desensitized to everything. What was one news story
that truly affected you and made you think differently about your own life? If none has,
pick a headline and run with it.

12. Put yourself as a character into any television, movie, or book medical drama. What do
you add to the hospital or private practice and what kind of medical knowledge have you
instilled your character with? Have fun with this one.

Name _____ Date _____

13. Talk about a time in which you avoided Western medicine and found a cure with alternative methods. Some of these methods might include herbal remedies, acupuncture, Qi Gong, etc. If you have never done anything like that, do a bit of research and craft a story involving such practices.

14. Create a character (or draw from your own experiences) with a chronic pain or illness that requires daily maintenance. How does it change his life and how does he keep a positive attitude throughout it all? Is a cure possible?

Name _____ Date _____

15. Talk about a time in which cancer affected your life or the lives of those around you. How would you deal with it if you were diagnosed yourself? I know this is a heavy one, but you can really get some good emotional material from such a prompt.

16. You have been given a magical healing ability to heal various wounds and illnesses. How do you go about implementing your power throughout your family and community?

Name _____ Date _____

17. Many people worry about what their health will be like in their old age. Describe an ideal day in the life for yourself when you are 80. Then describe one for 100 and 120 as well.

18. There is a glass scratching sound on your house's windows and you get up out of bed to check it out. You look toward the windows and don't see anything. All of the sudden the glass breaks and something jumps in! What is it and what do you do next?

Name _____ Date _____

19. You are a high school student in between classes. You open up your locker to find a severed head! The head has a note on it that says, "you're next!" What do you do and how do you avoid being next?

20. The zombie apocalypse has begun! Several people you know have already become zombies and now it's a game of survival. What do you do to make sure that you are one of the people left at the end of the movie?

Name _____ Date _____

21. You are on vacation with your friends in a strange place. One night, one of your friends disappears and you have a strange suspicion that he's been captured by something. What do you think happened and how do you get out of this situation alive?

22. You have been possessed by the devil! How do you deal with this and how do you make every effort to keep your soul possible? Feel free to go in a different direction from other possession movies.

Name _____ Date _____

23. If you had your choice of becoming any kind of vampire, which
one would it be? A Twilight vampire, a Buffy vampire, a True Blood vampire, etc.? Pick
one and tell your story of how you were turned and what resulted from that situation.

24. Write a story in which something extremely un-scary is terrorizing a small town. Try to
be original and avoid using things that have already been in other horror or horror comedy
stories. Have fun with it!

Name _____ Date _____

25. A friend of yours has had an ancient curse levied upon him.
What do you do to help and what happens to him throughout the curse?

26. Hell has been unleashed on earth and you are the key to stopping the horrible consequences. What do you do to reverse the problem and what was the reason that this hell descended upon the planet?

Name _____ Date _____

27. There are several evil spirits that have taken over your house and part of your neighborhood's block. How do you appease the spirits or get rid of them?

28. What aspects of your parents or guardians' education do you respect the most and why? Do you plan to exceed their level of education or not and why?

Name _____ Date _____

29. Imagine that you could plan out your best memories of high school, college and your adult life. What would these memories be and why? Tell the complete story from start to finish for at least one of them.

30. There is a good chance that you will make a new group of friends in college and/or your adult life. If you could use those new comrades to fill in the current social gaps of your life, what would these new pals be like and why?

Name _____ Date _____

31. If you could go out to lunch with yourself from five years in the future and yourself a decade down the line what would the three of you talk about? What would their best piece of advice be for you?

32. Imagine that you are going to a college so far away that there would be little chance that someone from your high school would attend with you. If you had the opportunity to bring one friend, one acquaintance and one other classmate to the school, who would they be and why?

Name _____ Date _____

33. One day, you may have a child and even a grandchild who will
also attend high school. What would your best piece of advice be to this descendent of
yours? How would this child or grandchild be similar and different to you?

34. In the movie of your high school experience, name the actors that would make up your
ideal cast. Make sure to include yourself, your parents, crush, friends and favorite teacher.

Name _____ Date _____

35. As technology changes, how do you think the high school experience will transform in the next 10 years, 30 years, 100 years?

36. Create a story about your ideal life 25 years from now. Include what you're doing for a living, who you live with, where you live and how well you're doing at achieving your goals.

Name _____ Date _____

37. While many teenagers tend to complain about what they don't have, there are people your age throughout the world with less food, money, shelter and education than you have. Write a list of things in your life that you're grateful for and write a story about how you'd deal without them. ribe a situation in which you were the coldest you've ever been in your life during the winter.

38. Think back to a time that you were extremely scared. What caused it, why did it make you so afraid and how did you let go of that fear? What would make you even more frightened today?

Name _____ Date _____

39. Remember a time in which you felt naive. What are some of the things you know now that you didn't know in that situation? Do you ever miss not having that knowledge, why or why not?

40. Have you ever been so excited that you could barely hold it in? Write about the experience and what it was that caused such anticipation. What would have to happen nowadays to give you the same level of excitement?

Name _____ Date _____

41. Create a story about a time in which you were happy to be alive. What caused this sensation and how much you be able to use this memory when you're feeling down?

42. Firsts are extremely important to us, such as losing our first tooth, our first day of school and our first kiss. Write about one of your firsts. What was so important about this first at the time and is it still important to you now?

Name _____ Date _____

43. You may remember your childhood as a laid back affair, but for
your parents or guardians it may have been a different story. Between dirty diapers, spit up
and sleepless nights, you may have been quite the handful. Write a story about a week in
your infancy from your parents or guardians' perspective.

44. Imagine a time in your life in which you were very embarrassed. Now imagine you
were 10 times as confident during the situation as you actually were. What would have
happened differently in the situation and why?

Name _____ Date _____

45. Write about a time in which someone made fun of you. How did you react and why? Do you wish you had handled the situation differently?

46. Imagine that you could switch lives with a friend, a loved one or a stranger for a day. Who would it be and why? Describe that day in different shoes from beginning to end.

Name _____ Date _____

47. What is the biggest goal in your life? Do you think that goal will change in the future or stay the same? How will you feel and what will you do if you ever achieve it?

48. In what was supposed to be a one-night vacation, you and every member of your extended family are trapped in a log cabin due to a snow storm that could day over a week to clear. How do you survive the bickering, the cooking and the abundance of tough love?

Name _____ Date _____

49. You have somehow been transported back to the day you first met "the one that got away." With a chance to do everything differently, can you succeed at true love?

50. The economic climate made the country ripe for takeover and a military coup has changed everything you've known in an instant. With rapid changes being instituted, how do you fit into a new regime full of violent transformation?

Name _____ Date _____

51. Place three characters from different time periods of your life
into the same room. Write a story about how they interact and what they say about you and
the kind of person you are..

52. Pick a town that you have lived in at some point during your life. Imagine that a major
event, anywhere from an alien landing to a harvest festival has occurred there. Craft a tale
of how the event has impacted the town using extreme detail.

Name _____ Date _____

53. In history class, it's difficult not to find a time period that really
resonates with you, whether it was the Italian Renaissance or the 1920's. Set a story in that
time period and play up all the elements you enjoy the most about it.

54. Create a small tale of a major event that happens over the course of one minute. Then,
try writing the same story over the course of one hour and then again over one day. Mix
the elements of the three stories into one tale set during a time length of your choice.

Name _____ Date _____

55. All technology has come crashing down and the Internet, computers and cell phones no longer work. While researchers attempt to determine the source of the problem, how will the world cope?

56. After winning a contest, you have the opportunity to meet your hero. The only issue is, this hero is nothing like the person you thought you were meeting. Describe the encounter from beginning to end. Is this person still your hero afterward?

Name _____ Date _____

57. Some strange occurrences in your life have led you to believe that everything you type on your computer turns into reality! How do you use this power and what are some of the things that happen during your typing frenzy?

58. You have shot up to superstardom through the ranks of the entertainment world and now you are hounded by the paparazzi every single day. How do you and your loved ones deal with this change?

Name _____ Date _____

59. You aren't a celebrity, but some how you landed a date with one!
What's it like going on a first date with cameras and autograph hounds continuously interrupting you?

60. A random YouTube video about a very political subject has become the most popular video in the world. People from both sides of the issue have come up to you on the street. What is the video about and what is your opinion about it?

Name _____ Date _____

61. Who is your favorite celebrity past or present and why? If you could do any activity with this person what would it be and why? Detail a story in which you are doing that.

62. You are in charge of a charity event and you have a major celebrity as your master of ceremonies. This MC is having some sort of problem (mentally or physically) that you need to help your celebrity with in order to make your charity event go well. Talk about your experiences.

Name _____ Date _____

63. What is the closest you've ever been to a celebrity (i.e. Jennifer Aniston bumped into me once) and how do you tell the story to your friends? If you don't have a situation like this, make one up.

64. With YouTube and reality TV, it seems like people are becoming celebrities for extremely silly reasons. Write about some "celebrities" that have gone down that path and what you believe the future holds for those folks.

Name _____ Date _____

65. Pick up a copy of a tabloid. Write some stories based on the ridiculous headlines held within.

66. If you were rich and famous how would you use your clout for charity? How would you use it for personal gain?

Name _____ Date _____

67. You have become known for a catch phrase that people repeat to
you every time they see you. Talk about a day in your life and how you cope with hearing
the same thing over and over again.

68. It's hot. Sticky hot. You are sitting in your house or apartment with broken air
conditioning and an outside temperature of 100 degrees F. Describe your day.

Name _____ Date _____

69. Ring a ling! It's the glorious Pavlov dog effect of the ice cream man. Write about your ice cream man experiences.

70. The old summer job… whether it be the snack counter at the local pool or a camp counselor at the day camp, we've all had them. Talk about yours in great detail.

Name _____ Date _____

71. Summer fling! Ever had one? If so, write about it, if not, make up your ideal summer relationship.

72. There are amazing family summer vacations and there are family summer vacation disasters. Pick one and have a ball with it.

Name _____ Date _____

73. Going to the beach or the pool to watch people walk by in their swimsuits. Detail an afternoon of lounging and people watching..

74. It is that week where all of your friends have gone out of town except for you. What do you do with your extreme free time?

Name _____ Date _____

75. Whether it's beach volleyball, soccer, or Frisbee, the summer can be filled with sports. What are some of your summer sports experiences?

76. What is your favorite summer dessert and why? Portray a very descriptive scene in which you devour your dessert. Write about every delicious bite.

Name _____ Date _____

77. You are suddenly transported to the middle of some unknown desert during the hottest part of the summer. How do you survive and get yourself to safety?

78. Take a time from your life (or imagine a time) that you were bullied at school. Who was the bully and how did he or she affect you? Imagine a sit down chat with the bully in which the person could not bully you and had to share his or her feelings. What do you think you would learn?

Name _____ Date _____

79. What was your shining school achievement? I there a moment
that you felt the most intelligent or the most gifted? Talk about that day, what led up to it,
and how it changed your life.

80. Talk about the teacher that you liked the most in school. What made you enjoy the
class that he or she taught and why was this person so memorable to the present day?

Name _____ Date _____

81. Talk about the teacher that you disliked the most in school. What was wrong with this person? If you had a chance to sit down with this teacher, what would you tell this person about how to change his or her teaching style (and perhaps attitude)?

82. Describe your first school crush or your first school significant other. What was it like? How did you feel walking around the school and possibly having people talk about you?

Name _____ Date _____

83. What is your favorite after-school activity? If you are a sports player, talk about that, a band member, talk about that, a chess club member, you get the idea. Describe how this activity makes you feel and why it was important to you at the time.

84. Talk about a time (or make up a time) in which you were called in to the principal or dean's office. What happened? Why were you there and what was the end result?

Name _____ Date _____

85. Who were your best friends in elementary school, middle school or high school? Talk about what you guys and gals used to do together and why you are no longer close or why you are still close to this very day. What was your most memorable school friend moment?

86. You have been sent back in time (to kindergarten) and you have the ability to change your entire schooling experience. How do you change the next 10 years of your life or so to make your life better? Does it work or do you lose some of the flavor along the way?

Name _____ Date _____

87. What has been your most awkward school experience ever? Write about it or make something up.

88. What is the best vacation you've ever been on? Who were you with? Where did you travel? What were some of the sights that you saw? Write down every detail and pose a hypothetical trip with the same people if you went back today.

Name _____ Date _____

89. What is the worst vacation you've ever been on? What fights occurred, how lost did you get, how much money did you lose, etc.? Pose a hypothetical of the trip going perfectly and see what major things would have changed.

90. What is your most memorable airport/airplane experience? Did you sit on the runway for a long time? Did you get to talk to someone interesting on the plane? Did you have to run really far to get to your gate on time? Use lots of details and try to remember all of the emotions that you had at the time.

Name _____ Date _____

91. Talk about a time in which you had to show someone foreign to
your neighborhood, town, country, or planet around the area. Do you feel as though you
were a good tour guide? What did this person (or alien) think after your demonstration?

92. Create a story in which you are in a foreign country in which you don't speak the
language...and you've lost all of your belongings (cash included). How do you deal with
this situation?

Name _____ Date _____

93. Why is travel so stressful? What would you have to do to take all
of the stress out of traveling for yourself? Perhaps a closer airport or calmer family
members? What if you owned your own jet? Talk about it as if it was happening and detail
your first stress-free traveling experience.

94. Did you ever have a friend from a foreign country? If not, make one up and talk about
how you met, what you learned and what it would be like if you lived in your friend's
native land.

Name _____ Date _____

95. Have you ever traveled back to the "mother country" to discover your family's roots? If not, make up a story in which you did and see how much you can find out about your ancestry. Did you learn anything about yourself and the kind of person you are on this trip?

96. Talk about a road trip that you've had. Who was there, where were you going, and what kind of rest stops did you stop at along the way? If you haven't been on such a trip, create the ideal trip for yourself by getting your best friends together and going to your favorite drivable location.

Name _____ Date _____

97. You are in the airport and you are about to travel home for the holidays. Except there's one problem: you're snowed in! Talk about your night (or nights) at the airport and if you meet any strange and interesting people.

98. You have been granted the ability to fly! I mean, like Superman! Where do you travel with this newfound ability now that you don't need to save up frequent flyer miles?

Name _____ Date _____

99. You have put together your dream travelling team of living and deceased people. Who are they and where do you go?

100. You wake up to find a post-it note attached to your forehead. This note is a clue that leads you to another clue somewhere in your house. Your family claims ignorance but they decide that they'll help you to solve the mystery. One clue continues to lead to another, where will it end?

Name _____ Date _____

101. There has been a murder and you are the top rated private eye in town. A mysterious woman who asks you to help with the case may also be the primary suspect. What is the evidence and how do you solve the case?

102. On a day that started like any other, your friends and family have started to treat you a bit strangely and you suspect that something is up. On a whim, you stay out a bit later then curfew. When you return your house is surrounded by police cars. What do you do?

Name _____ Date _____

103. You are the only eyewitness to a crime that even you don't truly understand. Both as witness protection and as an aid to the case, you team up with a special agent from the FBI. What was it you saw and how do you help to solve the crime together.

104. Someone has been stealing away the puppies from your town at night. You and a crack team of investigators (concerned people from the neighborhood and your friends) have decided to figure out the crime when the police can't. What do you do and how do you solve it?

Name _____ Date _____

105. Someone in your family's household has been stealing the
cookies from the cookie jar at night. You set up an elaborate surveillance system in order
to nab the culprit. Talk about you plan from beginning to end. Do you catch the thief?

106. Talk about a mystery that has occurred in your life. Start the story a bit before the
event and go through the future consequences. Was the mystery ever solved?

Name _____ Date _____

107. Have you ever been accused of a crime that you didn't commit (small or large)? Talk about the situation from both your side and the side of the lawmakers (who may be your parents or friends). What actually happened in the situation?

108. You have been transported into a world where everything plays out like film-noir. The world is black and white and you and your friends give monologues to the camera about what you're truly feeling. Talk about a day in the life of the mystery prone noir.

Name _____ Date _____

109. You are out camping in the forest and you wake to find your lucky hat missing. You and your friends must track down the perpetrator, whether man or animal. Use the clues of the forest (tracking, etc.) to find this wonderful head covering.

110. Recall and write a detailed account of your most embarrassing moment with your mother, step-mother, or other mother like figure.

Name _____ Date _____

111. Describe the time around the moment you realized that your mother and father were in fact not perfect or normal.

112. Write a story of your older brother or sister beating you up or you beating up a younger brother or sister. If it never happened, make it up.

©2012 Build Creative Writing Ideas

Name _____ Date _____

113. Describe this event: finding out the true nature of Santa Claus or the Easter Bunny and your first confrontation with your parents afterward.

114. In a detailed manner, write about the day of and the day after your little brother or sister was born. If you are an only child, imagine what it would be like.

Name _____ Date _____

115. Evaluate your place with your entire family. Are you the
starving artist? Maybe you're the slacker Or the underachieving genius? Label your role
and start labeling the other members of your family as well. Explain the labels.

116. Describe your most memorable family holiday/vacation.

Name _____ Date _____

117. Describe the first time you introduced a boyfriend or girlfriend to your immediate family.

118. Describe the first time you introduced a boyfriend or girlfriend to your extended family.

Name _____ Date _____

119. Use research or imagination to write a day in the life story of your mother, father or siblings when they were your current age.

120. In a "Freaky Friday"-esque situation, you have switched bodies with your mother or father. Describe your next 24 hours.

Name _____ Date _____

121. Write a story of one of your ancestors in connection to a famous event in history.

122. Think back to an event with your family from your childhood. Write a scene between you and a parent or sibling and try to piece together the whole event.

Name _____ Date _____

123. Either remember back to or imagine if your parents were to tell you that they were getting a divorce, describe your next 24 hours.

124. How did your sibling's reputation affect how teachers treated you in school (or vice versa)? Describe specific situations.

Name _____ Date _____

125. You have to spend a week with one cousin, who do you choose
and why? Describe the week. If you don't have a cousin, imagine spending a week with a
close friend or other family member.

126. You have to spend a week with one grandparent or one pair of grandparents. Who do
you choose and why? Describe the week.

Name _____ Date _____

127. Describe your family's greatest catastrophe to date.

128. Imagine or describe your own wedding and the involvement of your family in the planning and execution.

Name _____ Date _____

129. Your best friend in the world calls you and tells you a secret that changes your friendship forever. Describe the conversation and the aftermath.

130. Detail the scene of the first time you told your friends you had a crush on somebody. Did your friends react negatively or poorly? Did their reaction affect how you handled yourself around your crush?

Name _____ Date _____

131. The friend you that you had a falling out with knocks on your door. He or she comes in and you two sit down and talk about the old times and the new times. Write that conversation in dialogue form.

132. Your boyfriend or girlfriend for the past few months says that she or he does not want to ever hang out with your friends ever again. How do you handle the situation?

Name _____ Date _____

133. What is the craziest experience you've ever shared with your friends?

134. Look back in your life for a time when you had a bad breakup and you went to your friends for help. What happened?

Name _____ Date _____

135. You are asked to testify against a good friend of yours in a court case. Your friend is being tried for murder. You know full well that he committed it. What do you do?

136. Remember a time where two of your friends began to date. If this didn't happen, make up a story in which it did. How does it play out?

Name _____ Date _____

137. Your first major fight with a friend. The lead-up and the aftermath.

138. Your last major fight with your best friend. The lead-up and the aftermath.

Name _____ Date _____

139. Your friend is dating a horrible, horrible person. How do you deal with it? If this situation has happened in your life, feel free to draw from that.

140. You are lab partners with your friend in a science class. They're doing absolutely no work and this is bringing your grade down. How do you approach them about it?

Name _____ Date _____

141. A friend has borrowed a large sum of money from you and has yet to repay it. How do you approach the situation?

142. Your best friend calls you while crying up a storm. How do you comfort your friend and what is it probably about?

Name _____ Date _____

143. Describe meeting your best friend in the world.

144. In an ancient time, you are the personal writer to the King and Queen of your country. What do they require you to write and what is your day to day life like living in the castle?

Name _____ Date _____

145. How do you feel that writing will change 200 years in the future? 1,000 years in the future? If you lived during that time, with your predictions holding true, how would you thrive as a writer?

146. Seemingly overnight, the world has become completely obsessed with writing! The economy is now completely focused on writing, both imports and exports. Children have scorned television and Facebook to take up writing. How does this change your life and how does the future play out in this new writing world?

Name _____ Date _____

147. What would your writing have to accomplish for you to consider yourself a true success? Describe that accomplishment and where you would go from there?

148. John Milton wrote the epic poem "Paradise Lost" while he was blind. Describe how you would write such a masterpiece with a major disability. Would it be a driving force of motivation or more of a supreme hindrance?

Name _____ Date _____

149. Many people say that they've done everything they can when it comes to becoming a full-fledged writer. Write a story about a person who has actually done everything he or she can. This may include submitting manuscripts to publishers, writing an eBook, taking courses or anything else you can think of.

150. What is your favorite work of art about a writer? This can be a painting, a movie, a book, really anything at all. Write about how it impacts you as a writer.

Name _____ Date _____

151. What is your best quality as a writer and how did it become a part of your writing?

152. What is your worst quality as a writer and how did it become a part of your writing?

Name _____ Date _____

153. Name three attributes that you think would make you a much better writer if they were added to your persona. Talk about how you think you could obtain these new skills or traits.

154. Talk about three habits you have as a writer that you feel are a hindrance to your writing. How could you get rid of these or how do you think you could turn them into strengths?

Name _____ Date _____

155. If you had grand control over time, space and money, how would you change your life to suit your writing? Talk about a day in the life of this new writing-structured existence.

156. What is something in the world that inspires you to write? Why does it have this effect on you?

Name _____ Date _____

157. What is something in the world that makes you not want to write at all? What is it about this that makes you stop cold in your tracks?

158. What is the thing that you love the most about writing? Explain how it came to be this way.

Name _____ Date _____

159. What is an aspect of writing that you absolutely hate? Is there any way that you could make this aspect more fun and enjoyable?

160. If you could choose someone in history or someone living today to write a biography about, who would it be and why?

Name _____ Date _____

161. If you were teaching a child or a novice about writing, what are a few things that you would teach him or her and why?

162. If you could condense what your writing is "about" into one sentence, what would that be? Talk about why this explains your writing to a T.

Name _____ Date _____

163. How do you want your writing to affect people? Why? How does it affect people now?

164. Talk about a time in which you had to act in front of people, whether during a class presentation, a school play you were roped into, or in an off-Broadway production. It doesn't matter what it was, what matters for this prompt is to talk about how you felt and what you think the "audience" thought of your performance.

Name _____ Date _____

165. What is your favorite acting performance of all time: movie, television, stage play or other? Why was this performance so moving and why has it stuck with you?

166. You are stepping up to the podium for your first Academy Award speech (you won for Best Actor or Actress)! What do you say and who do you thank? Also, how does the post-show party go?

Name _____ Date _____

167. What was your worst acting experience? Did your pants split on stage or did the lines go completely out of your head? Were you totally off-key during a musical number or booed into oblivion? Talk about it and for fun write a version in which everything instead went right. If none of these things have ever happened to you, imagine what it would have been like and write about it.

168. You are in the cast of a well-received play or sketch comedy show. You have just found out that a big-time reviewer is going to be in the audience that night. How does it affect you and the rest of the cast? Does it change the way you decide to go about things?

Name _____ Date _____

169. You have just begun what was supposed to about a five minute scene during a packed house show. Your scene partner has forgotten all of his lines and is just looking at you as if he is mute. What do you to salvage the scene and save the show?

170. What kind of style of acting most appeals to you? Dissect a few of your experiences with all the styles you've encountered and decide on the one that's the most interesting to you.

Name _____ Date _____

171. Talk about a time in which you were so engrossed in the part you were acting that you were able to just let yourself run on autopilot. How did it go and what did you like or dislike about the experience?

172. You have been cast in a pilot for CBS! Who do you tell first? How do you get the word out to the rest of your friends? What are your experiences like shooting the first episode and getting officially picked up for a full-season run?

Name _____ Date _____

173. Describe a time in which you needed to act like somebody else in real life. Did you have to pretend to like somebody for a job? Did you have to act like you enjoyed a friend's parents company? Go into extreme detail.

174. List five people who you feel are constantly "putting on a show" and never revealing their true personalities. Put them in a room together and describe the experience.

Name _____ Date _____

175. You have the ability to create two new WWE superstars who will battle each other at the next PPV (wrestling talk for Pay Per View). What are their names, costumes, signature moves, and what is their overall persona like? Go into detail and then describe the feud and match from start to finish.

176. Talk about being a spectator at either a professional or scholastic wrestling match. What is the crowd like and what is the general feeling in the air? You can draw on personal experience or make it up, but make sure to go into extreme detail.

Name _____ Date _____

177. You come in for your early morning weigh-in the day of a meet
(your pre-match weigh in will be around 5 p.m.). You are 3 pounds over and you have no
idea how it happened? What happens next?

178. You go out to the mat and shake hands with your opponent. You're not exactly sure
how it happened, but the guy you're wrestling looks to be twice your size. Isn't that what
weight classes are for? How do you get through the six minute match?

©2012 Build Creative Writing Ideas

Name _____ Date _____

179. You have been given the position of a jobber in the WWE.
What is a jobber? A wrestler who goes out there to lose to the big stars so that audience is happy. How do you deal with going in, losing, and collecting your paycheck just to lose again? Talk about a week in the life of your jobber career.

180. Somehow, you have been transported into the body of a huge muscle head in the midst of the 1980s. This muscle head is in a WWF old-school feud with the most famous wrestler of all time. What do you and this icon talk about in the middle of your match? How does it feel to be wrestling one of the greats in the midst of his prime?

Name _____ Date _____

181. You go out to the mat to meet your opponent. It's a girl! While,
this isn't completely unheard of, it's the first time that you've ever had to wrestle a girl. You look over and see the snickering of your friends. What happens in the match?

182. Some people think that losing weight for a wrestling match is only steps away from an eating disorder. What is your opinion on the matter? Do you think that wrestling is unhealthy, why or why not?

Name _____ Date _____

183. You are in the big shower with a bunch of other wrestlers after a big practice. You are having your typical conversation about sports and gross guy stuff. Detail the conversation from beginning to end.

184. Your favorite wrestling super star has selected you in a contest to go out with him to a club and hang out for the entire night. How does the night go? What are all the crazy weird things he tells you about his life?

Name _____ Date _____

185. You have inherited your own amateur wrestling federation.
What kind of wrestlers do you work with and how do you rival the huge monopolized WWE?

186. Create your dream wrestling match between two superstars who lived in different eras. Describe the match in extreme detail.

Name _____ Date _____

187. You have unintentionally achieved the proverbial American
Dream; you have two kids, a white picket fence, a nice house, and a loving spouse. Work
on a sort of timeline of how your next 30-50 years turn out with this situation.

188. What does the American Dream mean to you? What do you feel is your American
Dream and how do you want to end up living?

Name _____ Date _____

189. Is the American Dream still about living comfortably with a family or is it now about living in extreme wealth and getting to do pretty much whatever you want? Cite some examples and perhaps even a back and forth between two families.

190. What would you consider to be success in American society? What would be failure? What would have to happen for you to be willing to compromise your vision of success?

Name _____ Date _____

191. Create a hypothetical story in which a large world event changes the American Dream drastically for the better or the worse. Go into extreme detail and perhaps tell the story from several different perspectives.

192. How do you feel the American Dream compares to the "Dream" in other countries? In comparison to them, do we set our standard too high or too low? Or is the American Dream completely off? Go into detail.

Name _____ Date _____

193. Family is a huge part of the American Dream. How does your family compare to one of a healthy marriage, with two kids, and a dog? Where do you believe that puts you in society?

194. You have achieved the American Dream but it isn't as fulfilling as you thought it would be? How do you become satisfied with what you have or how do you end up achieving more?

Name _____ Date _____

195. Talk about a movie, book, or television show in which a family attempts to achieve success in America. What lessons can you learn from their journey and what things could they have done differently? Write your own story of a family attempting the same sort of thing.

196. You are granted a window into the future about 20 years. How do you and your family place in American society in that time? Have you gone up or down or stayed the same? Knowing what you know from that vision and that the future most definitely can be changed, what will you do?

Name _____ Date _____

197. Imagine that you are part of a family of immigrants arriving at
Ellis Island with a head full of dreams. How do you and your family survive and thrive?

198. You sit up in bed and you see a ghost of one of your deceased relatives. Who is it and
what is it they say to you? Does anyone else see this paranormal phenomenon?

Name _____ Date _____

199. Talk about an experience in which you felt an other-worldly presence. If you do not have one, make one up or talk about how a real life experience might have been influenced by some kind of ghost.

200. How would people live differently if they knew they were always going to hang around as ghosts? How would people's opinions about death change and what would they do with their ghostly afterlives?

Extra Page

Name _____ Date _____